Presented to:

_____

*The loveliest masterpiece of the heart of God
is the heart of a mother.*

SAINT THERESE OF LISIEUX

Presented by:

_____

Date:

_____

Celebrate Mom

Heartwarming Stories,
Inspirational Sayings, and
Loving Expressions
for a Special Mother

WHITE STONE BOOKS
LAKELAND, FLORIDA

Celebrate Mom:
Heartwarming Stories, Inspirational Sayings, and Loving Expressions
for a Special Mother

ISBN: 1-59379-060-0

Copyright © 2006 Bordon Books, Tulsa, OK
Published by White Stone Books
P.O. Box 2835
Lakeland, Florida 33806

Manuscript written and prepared by SnapdragonEditorialGroup℠.

Contents

Dissect a mother's heart and see

The properties it does contain—

What pearls of love.

What gems of hope.

A mother's heart beats not in vain.

CALEB DUNN

Introduction

Motherhood is one of the strongest bonds known to humankind and certainly one of the most fulfilling. But if you're a mother, you already know what it takes to keep a "mother's heart" going—an endless fountain of love, patience, kindness, and forgiveness; fervent prayer and the ability to fight spiritual battles; strong reserves of hope and faith; and a constant renewal of strength, courage, and determination.

Whether you have been a mother for many years or you are looking forward to the birth of your first child, *Celebrate Mom* was designed to inspire, encourage, and applaud the special "heart" God has placed in you—a heart fashioned after His own.

A Mother's Heart Is Filled with Love

There is in this cold and hollow world no fount of deep, strong, deathless love, save that within a mother's heart.

FELICIA HEMANS
British Poet
1793-1835

Love for spouse and friends pale in the light of a mother's love for her child. It is a love like no other, because it's an endowment from God. Without it, you would not be able to be covenant protector of another's body, mind, and soul. When you feel stretched tight, remind yourself that God loves you even more. Ask Him to refill your mother's heart once again to overflowing.

Love covers all offenses.

PROVERBS 10:12 NRSV

A mother's love is indeed the golden link
that binds youth to age; and he is still but a child, however
time may have furrowed his check,
or silvered his brow, who can yet recall,
with a softened heart, the fond devotion,
or the gentle chidings, of the best friend
God ever gives us.

CHRISTIAN NESTELL BOVEE
American Author
1820-1904

Mother Love

Love of our mothers living yet,

In cradle song and bedtime prayer,

In nursery rhyme and fireside lore,

Thy presence still pervades the air;

Love of our mother, priceless gift,

Our grateful hearts thy praise uplift.

Love of our mothers, tender love,

The fount of childhood's trust and grace,

Oh, may thy consecration prove

The wellspring of a nobler race;

Love of our mothers, priceless gift,

Our grateful hearts thy praise uplift.

AUTHOR UNKNOWN

God's Heart for Mothers Is Filled with Love

His love for you ...

❃ *is unconditional,* just as you will always love your children with a profound, unconditional love, "God demonstrates his own love for us in this: While we were still sinners, Christ died for us" (Romans 5:8).

❃ *endures forever.* As a mother, from your heart burns a flame of everlasting love that nurtures and renews the heart of the child seeking reassurance, and in this we "give thanks to the LORD, for he is good. His love endures forever" (Psalm 136:1).

❃ *cannot be taken away.* There is nothing your children could ever do to take your love. This unspeakable love is an eternal gift from the very day God places a child in a mother's life. And so it is that "neither death nor life, neither angels nor demons, neither the present nor the future, nor any powers, neither height nor depth, nor anything else in all creation, will be able to separate us from the love of God that is in Christ Jesus our Lord" (Romans 8:38-39).

❃ *is vast.* A mother's love is one of the deepest loves that can be experienced, but even deeper is the love God has for you as His own child. "I pray that you, being rooted and established in love, may have power, together with all the saints, to grasp how wide and long and high and deep is the love of Christ, and to know this love that surpasses knowledge" (Ephesians 3:17-19).

There is no love on earth, I think,
as potent and enduring
as a mother's love for her child.

ANN KIEMEL ANDERSON
Christian Author and Speaker

Everyone who loves has been born of God
and knows God.

1 JOHN 4:7

A Tribute to My Mother

My mother's love has been one of the few constants in my life. It seems that I'm always in her thoughts. When I call, she tells me she's been praying for me. When I see her, she still takes me in her arms and holds me tight. Her face lights up when I tell her of my simple accomplishments, and she always gives me her full attention whenever I need to talk to someone. She believes in me, more than anyone I've ever known.

Lord, I thank You for allowing me to be the recipient of such love. And I ask that You would show me how best to love her in return. Show me how to pray for her and believe in her and sacrifice for her as she has for me. Show me how to be the grateful child of a loving mother.

Anya's Gift of the Heart

My eleventh birthday was a week away when we arrived at the refugee camp in Austria on that cold November day in 1947. My grandparents and I had fled our Soviet-occupied country of Hungary with only the clothes we were wearing.

To frightened, cold, and hungry people like us, the displaced persons camp was a blessing from God. We were given our own little cardboard-enclosed cubicle in a barrack, fed hot soup, and supplied with warm clothes. We had much to be grateful for. But as for my upcoming birthday, I didn't even want to think about it. We had left Hungary without possessions or money, but we were still alive. That was the important thing. So I put birthday presents and celebrations behind me.

My Anya was the only mother I had ever known because her only child, my mother, had died suddenly when I was just a few weeks old. Before World War II intensified, my birthdays had been grand celebrations with many cousins in attendance and lots of gifts.

My eighth birthday had been the last time I received a store-bought gift. Times were already hard then, money was scarce, and survival was our utmost goal. But my Anya had managed to pawn something, so she could buy me a book. I loved it! *Cilike's Adventures*, a wonderful book full of humor and adventure, had transported me many times from the harshness of the real world to a world of laughter and fun.

On November 25, when I awoke in our cardboard cubicle, I laid there and thought about being eleven. I was practically a grown-up, I told myself, and I would act accordingly when my grandparents Anya and Apa awoke. I didn't want them to feel bad because they couldn't give me a present. So I dressed quickly and tiptoed out as quietly as possible. I ran across the frosty dirt road to the barrack marked "women's bathroom and shower," washed, combed my hair, and finally returned to our cardboard sleeping quarters.

"Good morning, sweetheart! Happy birthday," Apa greeted me cheerily.

"Thank you, Apa, but I'd just as soon forget about birthdays from now on." I squirmed in his generous hug.

"You are too young to forget about birthdays," Anya said. "Besides, who would I give this present to if birthdays are to be forgotten?"

"Present?" I looked at her in surprise as she reached into her pocket and pulled something out.

"Happy birthday, sweetheart. It's not much of a present, but I thought you might like having Cilike back on your eleventh birthday," she said, tears welling up in her eyes.

"My old Cilike book! But I thought we left it behind," I said. I hugged the book to my chest while tears of joy flowed down my cheeks.

"Well, it almost was," Anya said. "But when we had to leave so quickly in the middle of the night, I grabbed it, along with my prayer book, and stuck it in my pocket. I knew how much you loved that book, so I couldn't bear to leave it behind. I'm sorry it's not a new book, but I hope you like having it back."

"Oh, thank you, Anya! Having Cilike back means so much to me. So very much." I hugged her again. "It's the best birthday present I have ever received!"

And it was, because I realized that day that God had blessed me with a wonderful mother, whose love would always see me through the hard times. She taught me that gifts of the heart are always the best gifts, because they truly are gifts of love.[1] ♥

*Who is it that loves me and
will love me forever with an affection
which no chance, no misery,
no crime of mine can do away?
It is you, my mother.*

THOMAS CARLYLE
Scottish Essayist and Historian
1795-1881

Because I feel that

In the Heavens above,

The angels, whispering

To one another,

Can find, among their

Burning terms of love, none so devotional as

That of "Mother."

Therefore by that dear

Name I long have

Called you.

EDGAR ALLAN POE
Poet and Gifted Writer of American Literature
1809-1849

A Mother's Heart Is Strong and Courageous

No language can express the power and beauty
and heroism of a mother's love.

EDWIN H. CHAPIN
Poet and Songwriter
1814-1880

I'm just a simple woman—in essence that's what Mary said when she learned she would be the mother of the Christ Child. If you're a mother, you've been there, cowering at the immensity of the task. You're right to be concerned. Being a mother requires strength and courage in amounts that you might not be able to find in yourself. But God has all you'll ever need. Ask Him to make your mother's heart tough and brave.

I can do everything through him
who gives me strength.

PHILIPPIANS 4:13

Before you were conceived I wanted you.
Before you were born I loved you.
Before you were here an hour I would die for you.
This is the miracle of life.

MAUREEN HAWKINS
Author

God's Heart for Mothers
Is Strong and Courageous

He ...

⚜ *works on your behalf.* As a mother continually looks out for the welfare of her children, "the eyes of the LORD run to and fro throughout the whole earth, to show Himself strong on behalf of those whose heart is loyal to Him" (2 Chronicles 16:9 NKJV).

⚜ *strengthens, helps, and upholds you.* God's heart is like the heart of a mother, longing to comfort and to care for His children. "Fear not, for I am with you; be not dismayed, for I am your God. I will strengthen you, yes, I will help you, I will uphold you with My righteous right hand" (Isaiah 41:10 NKJV).

⚜ *defeated your enemy, the devil.* The love of God is a powerful force, strong and courageous on your behalf. "Having disarmed the powers and authorities, he made a public spectacle of them, triumphing over them by the cross" (Colossians 2:15).

⚜ *overcame death for you.* Because Jesus overcame sin and death on the cross, "death has been swallowed up in victory. Where, O death, is your victory? Where, O death, is your sting?" (1 Corinthians 15:54-55).

⚜ *makes your children mighty.* Because you are a mother who fears the Lord and teaches His ways to your children, they will be blessed by God! "Happy are those who fear the LORD, who greatly delight in his commandments. Their descendants will be mighty in the land" (Psalm 112:1-2 NRSV).

Mother's Way

Sometimes when our hearts grow weary,

Or our task seems very long;

When our burdens look too heavy,

And we deem the right all wrong,

Then we gain a new, fresh courage,

As we rise to proudly say:

"Let us do our duty bravely

This, you know, was mother's way."

AUTHOR UNKNOWN

A Tribute to My Mother

As long as I can remember, my mother has smiled through the difficult times—she calls it being strong for her children. Even now, she is determined to shield us from trouble if she can. When I got a little older, I scoffed at her always upbeat attitude, thinking she was simply refusing to face reality. But then one day, I heard her asking You for strength and courage—enough for herself and more to share with her children.

Now I understand, Lord, that my mother was not denying the problem or smiling through her fears. Her smile came from the courage and strength she received from You.

I want to be that kind of parent to my children, Lord. I ask that You would infuse me with Your strength and bolster me with Your courage so that I, too, might be a rock of refuge for my family.

Mother's Courageous Journey

As my husband, Bob, and I drove from Kansas City to St. Louis suburbs, eagerness to see my mother welled up in my heart. Then waves of uneasiness. *So much has changed*, I thought. Mother, widowed and now ninety, suffered from pain and disabilities. She required caregivers around the clock. She fought one of life's tough journeys—declining health.

As I approached the back door, I gazed at the acre surrounding her ranch home. It was a beautiful yard full of tall trees, evergreens, a birdbath, and flower boxes. A large pot with pink impatiens swayed from an elm. Warmth filled me to see my childhood home—a heavenly place. But Mother would no longer scurry to the door to greet us.

I breathed a prayer as we went inside. Mother sat in a chair, looking her best. She wore make-up and her styled auburn hair was colored just right. She wore an aqua dress with a necklace and matching earrings. Her smile radiated joy to see us. Immediately she stretched out her arms.

We hugged and kissed, and I handed her fresh red carnations.

"They're beautiful! Thank you," she said.

Again I studied her. *Mom isn't giving up*, I thought. I knew she had used limited strength to dress nicely—especially today.

My twin sister, Alberta, who lived nearby, came often and helped Mother in many ways. Alberta told me what special "mother-daughter" times they had. Now it was my turn. I wanted to do all I could to help Mother in practical ways and to express my love.

I had also come to be blessed and refreshed by my Christian mother even in her pain and weakness. Many adults won't admit it, but we still need our mothers' love and affirmation.

When the caregiver left, I took over, fixing Mother a snack and attending to her needs. She asked about our lives and about her grandchildren. Right away, she fed me with her love.

"How are you doing, really?" I asked.

"Some days the pain is terrible," she said. "And I feel so trapped. I can't get around in my own house without someone pushing me in the wheelchair. I would love to bake a cake or garden—the things I used to do. When people get to my age, it's one loss after another." Then her eyes brightened. "But God is in charge. He sees me through."

I took her hand and looked into her eyes. "Mother, I can see now that one of the most courageous things we'll ever do is to face getting old—and meeting challenges like you have. You are doing it through God's grace. I admire you."

Then I remembered a quote she had sent me years back. Misty-eyed I reminded her of the words: "Each day is a little life. Fill its hours with gladness if you can;

with courage if you can't."

"That's you, Mother. You are still teaching me how to live."

"Thank you, honey," she said. "It's God's strength."

Each day Bob and I spent with Mother, she told stories of when Alberta, Wally, and I were under her wing. She rambled some, but her mind was amazingly clear. "I loved being a homemaker—that's all I ever wanted to be," she affirmed. We talked about God's purposes and what counts in life, and that meant so much to me.

My heart ached to watch Mother struggle with simple tasks. With failing eyesight, it took her a long time to scribble a note on a birthday card. But she finished it.

When it was time to return to Kansas City, I sat with Mother as she rested on her bed. At her request, I took her hand in mine and prayed for her. I thanked God for a wonderful mother.

Is this my last time with her? I wondered. Tears blurred my vision as we drove away. Fortunately, we had two more years of visits, and we spoke by phone often. One Christmas Mother gave me a white cotton throw comforter. She wrote a note in large letters: "Dear Daughter, Charlotte—When you are weary and cold, wrap up in this with my love and you will be refreshed. Much love, Mother."[2] ❤

I have been told that my mother, when she surmised from the face of the physician that her life and that of her child could not both be saved, begged him to spare the child. So through these many years of mine, I have seldom thanked God for His mercies without thanking Him for my mother.

JAMES M. LUDLOW
American General
1758-1842

She is just an extraordinary mother and a gentle person. I depended on her for everything. I watched her become a strong person. And that had an enormous influence on me.

ROSALYNN CARTER
Wife of Former President James Carter

A Mother's Heart Is Kind and Nurturing

The woman who creates and sustains a home and under whose hands children grow up to be strong and pure men and women, is a creator second only to God.

HELEN (MARIA FISKE) HUNT JACKSON
American Writer
1830-1885

God is a nurturer. He looks after those He loves— nourishes them, guides and protects them, and nudges them toward growth and maturity. As a mother, you have been created like Him in that regard. Your mother's heart is a nurturing heart. All you need to succeed as a mother is to give your children what God has given you: lots of love, lots of kindness, lots of forgiveness, lots of time together.

Above all else, guard your heart,
for it is the wellspring of life.

PROVERBS 4:23

Countless times each day a mother does what no one else
can do quite as well. She wipes away a tear,
whispers a word of hope, eases a child's fear.
She teaches, ministers, loves, and nurtures
the next generation of citizens.
And she challenges and cajoles her kids to do their best and
be the best. But no editorials praise these accomplishments—
where is the coverage our mothers rightfully deserve?

JAMES. C. DOBSON
Christian Psychologist, Author, and Radio Teacher

AND GARY L. BAUER
American Politician and Family Values Advocate

What Makes a Home

A man can build a mansion
Anywhere this world about,
A man can build a palace
Richly furnish it throughout.

A man can build a mansion
Or a tiny cottage fair,
But it's not the hallowed place called
"Home"
'Til Mother's dwelling there.

A man can build a mansion
With a high and spacious dome,
But no man in this world can build
That precious thing called "Home."

A man can build a mansion
Carting treasures o'er the foam,
Yes, a man can build the building
But Mother makes it "Home."

AUTHOR UNKNOWN

God's Heart for Mothers Is Kind and Nurturing

He ...

* *draws you by His loving-kindness.* God's love, like a mother's love, is filled with kindness toward His children. "I have loved you with an everlasting love; I have drawn you with loving-kindness" (Jeremiah 31:3).

* *never forgets you.* A mother's heart is always turned toward her children, and God's heart is always turned toward you. "Can a mother forget the baby at her breast and have no compassion on the child she has borne? Though she may forget, I will not forget you!" (Isaiah 49:15).

* *covers you.* Your own mother heart springs from the eternal heart of God, who longs to shelter and care for His own. "Like an eagle that rouses her chicks and hovers over her young, so he spread his wings to take them in and carried them aloft on his pinions" (Deuteronomy 32:11 NLT).

* *will encourage you.* God brings you the encouragement you need this day to be the mother He has called you to be. "He will not break the bruised reed, nor quench the dimly burning flame. He will encourage the faint-hearted, those tempted to despair" (Isaiah 42:3 TLB).

A kind heart is a fountain of gladness,
making everything in its vicinity
freshen into smiles.

WASHINGTON IRVING
American Author
1783-1859

Your greatest pleasure is
that which rebounds from hearts
that you have made glad.

HENRY WARD BEECHER
Eloquent, Dramatic, and Witty Protestant Preacher
1813-1887

A Tribute to My Mother

Thank You for a mother who was always there for me. Even though she was at work when I got home from school, I always felt her presence. Cookies left out on the counter, a note taped to the TV screen, a smiley face stuck to my favorite drink in the fridge. Even when she didn't have time for special things, she never missed our afternoon phone call—just to chat for a couple of minutes about school, dinner, stuff.

I ask, Lord, that You would make me just as aware of her needs now as she was of my needs then. Help me to remember to pray for her every day, to call in the afternoon just to talk, and to be to her a fountain of encouragement. And for those acts of kindness that I can't repay, I ask that Your hand of blessing would be on her.

Out of the Nest

I knew something was wrong when I heard the frantic chirping outside. My eight-year-old daughter Michelle and I ran around the side of the house and saw a beautiful pair of cardinals swooping around their baby. It sat on the ground, peeping as loudly as its tiny lungs could bellow.

My daughter, who dearly loves all living things, squealed as a neighbor's dog bounded into our yard. We scrambled to save the cardinal chick while the neighbor kids tugged at their dog's leash.

"We rescued the baby!" my daughter shouted proudly to our neighbor, who was mowing his grass. Once again I was a hero in her eyes. It was the second time in a year I had saved a baby bird.

Patiently, I made phone calls to local wildlife refuges, bird rehabilitators, and veterinarians. They encouraged us to put the bird into a basket and place it in a tree to let the parents care for it.

I searched my collection of baskets for the tallest one, transferred the cheeping bird, and watched as my husband wedged it into the fork of the tree where the parents sat, waiting and watching. Within seconds the feathered baby bird had hopped to the edge of the basket. He leapt earthward, his tiny wings fluttering long enough to settle into the middle of the road.

Another frantic scramble ensued, and we rescued the bird again. I looked into its tiny, peeping face and wondered why the creature felt compelled to wander from the nest when he obviously wasn't ready to fly the distance. Why did that baby bird insist on independence over parental watchfulness? Thunderstorms were predicted for the night so Cheep found temporary shelter in my office.

The next morning, I called a wildlife store. The manager explained that we should return the chick outside for the parents to care for on the ground. If we tried to raise it, the bird would probably die when we set it free. It needed nurturing from its parents who would teach the bird to find food, water, and shelter.

"They even teach him how to waterproof his feathers," he explained.

Michelle wept as we set the baby bird free. We watched in fascination as the mother cardinal swooped down to the chick and then flew away. Over and over she came and went, always leaving in the same direction. The baby followed as best it could. Finally, it stopped to rest in the grassy shade of a tree.

Mom and Dad Cardinal never left their post in that tree, coming down to feed their baby occasionally. Once a loud raucous noise brought us outside again to see a desperate fight between Daddy Cardinal and a large blue jay. We marveled at the way the parents cared for and protected the lost bird, unwilling to abandon it.

Hours later, they were gone. We could only hope the baby was able to take wing and follow its parents to a safer place.

I couldn't help but see the parallel. As they grow, our human children also like to try out their wings and seem determined to leave the nest—often before they are ready. When they do, it can be difficult trying to guide and nurture and protect outside of our comfort zones. But we do it anyway, because that's the way God made us. I'm a mother. I'll breathe easier once I see my daughter confidently spread her wings and take flight. But until then, I'll do what mothers do.[3] ❤

Momma was the most totally human, human being that I have ever known; and so very beautiful. Within our home, she was an abundance of love, discipline, fun, affection, strength, tenderness, encouragement, understanding, inspiration, support.

LEONTYNE PRICE
World-Renowned Soprano

Home Is Where Mother Is

A child was asked,

"Where is your home?"

The little fellow replied,

"Where mother is."

Ah, there is home—

"Where mother is."

AUTHOR UNKNOWN

A Mother's Heart Is Filled with Wisdom

Wisdom from God shows itself
most clearly in a loving heart.

LLOYD JOHN OGILVIE
Author and Retired Chaplain of the U.S. Senate

One mother might call it instinct, another experience, but the Bible calls it wisdom. It's that inner understanding that comes after you've prayed for your child. Somehow you know what to do, how to respond, which words and actions will comfort the hurt, defuse the anger, clear the confusion. It's what makes you the very best person to help or advise your child—young or old—and it's God's gift. All you have to do is ask.

If any of you is lacking in wisdom,
ask God, who gives to all generously and
ungrudgingly, and it will be given you.
But ask in faith, never doubting.

JAMES 1:5-6 NRSV

*Don't expect wisdom to come into your life
like great chunks of rock on a conveyor belt.
It isn't like that. It's not splashy and bold,
nor is it dispensed like a prescription across a
counter. Wisdom comes privately from God
as a by-product of right decisions, godly
reactions, and the application of spiritual
principles to daily circumstances.*

CHARLES SWINDOLL
American Author and Bible Teacher

God's Heart Is Filled with Wisdom

His wisdom …

❀ *is superior to earthly wisdom.* The wisdom of a mother is much like the wisdom of God, and it springs from the heart of God. "The wisdom that comes from heaven is first of all pure; then peace-loving, considerate, submissive, full of mercy and good fruit, impartial and sincere" (James 3:17).

❀ *founded the world.* The whole earth is full of God's wisdom—all of the answers that you seek can be found in Him. "God made the earth by his power; he founded the world by his wisdom" (Jeremiah 10:12).

❀ *has been stored up for you.* Even as your mother's heart longs for wisdom in the matters of your children, God has already stored up all of the wisdom you will ever need. "He will be the sure foundation for your times, a rich store of salvation and wisdom and knowledge" (Isaiah 33:6).

❀ *is generously given to you.* What answers do you need today? How reassuring it is to know that "if any of you lacks wisdom, he should ask God, who gives generously to all without finding fault, and it will be given to him" (James 1:5).

Mother's Wisdom

At the age of 4, I thought: My mommy can do anything!

At the age of 8, I thought: My mom is the smartest mom.

At the age of 12, I thought: My mom doesn't know everything.

At the age of 14, I thought: My mom doesn't have a clue!

At the age of 16, I thought: Someone needs to fill that woman in.

At the age of 18, I thought: My mom is completely out of touch.

At the age of 25, I thought: As a last resort, I think I'll ask Mom.

At the age of 35, I thought: I've got to talk to Mother first.

At the age of 45, I thought: My mom is the wisest woman I know.

At the age of 70, I thought: If only I could ask Mother!

AUTHOR UNKNOWN

Heavenly Father:

I want to always be there for my children. Sometimes it is so difficult to know what to say and what to do to help my children put things into the right perspective. I want to balance my children's longing for independence and their need to have someone help them make the tough choices.

Lord, I need Your wisdom—the kind that only comes from You. Your Word tells me that You give generously to all those who ask for it—and I'm asking. Give me that right word at the right time for my children. And show me how best to guide them toward the plan You have established for their lives. It's a big request, and I give You my earnest thanks for Your answer.

Amen.

Score One for Mom

I was surprised to hear Emily's voice on the other end of the line. My fourteen-year-old daughter had been given permission to attend a small pizza party after school on Friday at her friend Emma's house, and I didn't expect to hear from her until later that evening. Why was she calling after being there less than an hour? Was she okay? Was someone hurt?

"Hi, Mom," she said lightly. "Um-m-m … Emma wants me to stay overnight."

There was nothing unusual about the words, but I sensed a veiled urgency in her tone. Being a mother of four girls, I was well aware how giggly and noisy teenagers can be, but while I could hear all that in the background, it definitely wasn't in her voice. Following God's leading, I started asking questions, and the short conversation went something like this:

Mom: This sounds like you want me to tell you no. Is that the case?

Emily: Uh-huh.

Mom: May I assume that her parents are not going to be home after all?

Emily: Right.

Mom: And the group has gotten much larger?

Emily: Yeah, pretty much so.

Mom: And you're uncomfortable with what you see ahead for the evening?

Emily: Very.

Mom: Is Emma standing close to you?

Emily: At this moment, yes … very.

Mom: Well, I'm happy to be the bad guy. So since we're going to Grandma's tomorrow, I think you'd better come home and clean your room and finish your chores. You won't have any other time over the weekend. Now you can show your token disappointment.

Emily: Aw, c'mon, Mom! I'll have time! Why can't I do it when we get back? It can't take me more than an hour!

Mom: So you're telling me that the pizza has been ordered and that I should pick you up in an hour, is that right?

Emily: Okay, fine then!

I smiled as I hung up the phone and felt a wave of gratitude for God's wisdom—that I had tuned in to my daughter's desperate need for me to hear what she wasn't saying.

An hour later I pulled into the driveway of the fancy house and did the very thing that is one of my major pet peeves: I honked the horn. I'm a firm believer that vehicle horns are for warnings only—for other cars who are about to hit you or people you are about to hit—not for letting someone know you have arrived. However, I knew that going to the door would force Emily's friend to lie about where her parents were.

My daughter rushed out with a convincing stomp, turned to wave at her friend, and shrugged her shoulders as if to say, "Sorry. You know how parents can be."

A block away, she leaned over and kissed my cheek and said, "Thanks, Mom! I'm so glad you 'heard' me. I really didn't want to be there—more and more kids were coming in and they were bringing beer and other stuff. They already think I'm a 'goody two shoes' so I couldn't just say I was leaving. I'm disappointed in Emma, though. She lied to me, and she lied to her parents."

We talked about the incident a lot that night, and we have talked about it and similar situations over the years. We talk about trusting God's leading and that He will give us wisdom to do the right thing. We talk about her absolute assurance that I'm there for her no matter what. We talk about the benefits of knowing right from wrong. We talk about not letting other people make important choices for us or holding them up on some jaded pedestal. We talk about having open dialogue even when it's painful or when we don't agree.

Emily is now a mother of three young children, and what a thrill it is to see her use wisdom to rescue her own kids from situations where they feel uncomfortable or frightened.

Once her children were watching a video at a friend's house intended to keep them entertained while the adults visited. While the host's children were completely "into it," Emily's kids slowly moved farther and farther away from the screen.

Emily noticed and said, "You know, guys, it's okay if you'd rather color or draw or play a game until the video is over." The look of relief on their little faces was unforgettable. Score one for motherly wisdom. It's a God thing![4] ♥

*I understood the value of having a mother
who had not stopped taking chances and
looking at life with delight.
It was comforting to know that I was not at the
head of the parade, that there was an older,
wiser woman moving in front of me.*

PHYLLIS THEROUX
Essayist, Columnist, Teacher, and Author

God grant me the serenity
To accept the things I cannot change,
The courage to change the things I can,
And the wisdom to know
One from the other.

REINHOLD NIEBUHR
Prominent American Theologian
1892-1971

Most mothers are instinctive philosophers.

HARRIET BEECHER STOWE
Author of *Uncle Tom's Cabin*
1811-1896

*In bringing up children, what good mothers
instinctively feel like doing for their babies
is usually best after all.*

BENJAMIN SPOCK
Pediatrician and Best-Selling Author
1903-1998

A Mother's Heart Is Patient and Understanding

*Life is the first gift, love is the second,
and understanding is the third.*

AUTHOR UNKNOWN

Give me patience, Lord, and give it to me NOW. That's a request any mother could get behind, regardless of whether her children are young or old. Fortunately, God has demonstrated His willingness to honor such requests. He will give you patience on the spot if you need it—and with it, He will give you understanding. That means you will have even more resources to help you handle the challenges ahead.

Be patient, bearing with one another in love.

EPHESIANS 4:2

A mother is the truest friend we have, when trials, heavy and sudden, fall upon us; when adversity takes the place of prosperity; when friends who rejoice with us in our sunshine, desert us when troubles thicken around us, still will she cling to us, and endeavor by her kind precepts and counsels to dissipate the clouds of darkness, and cause peace to return to our hearts.

WASHINGTON IRVING

American Author

1783-1859

A mother's love is patient and forgiving

When all others are forsaking.

And it never fails or falters,

Even though the heart is breaking.

HELEN STEINER RICE

Called the Poet Laureate of Inspirational Verse

1900-1981

A Mother's Prayer

Lord, give me patience when wee hands

Tug at me with their small demands.

Give me gentle and smiling eyes;

Keep my lips from hasty replies.

Let not weariness, confusion, or noise

Obscure my vision of life's fleeting joys.

So, when in years to come my house is still—

No bitter memories its rooms may fill.

Amen.

AUTHOR UNKNOWN

God's Heart for Mothers Is Patient and Understanding

His patience ...

- *gives you the opportunity to turn toward Him.* Is there anything more patient than a mother's love? Her heart demonstrates that "the Lord is not slow in keeping his promise, as some understand slowness. He is patient with you, not wanting anyone to perish, but everyone to come to repentance" (2 Peter 3:9).

- *prevents Him from being easily angered at you.* A mother's patience is boundless, especially as she allows the patience of the Lord to shine through her life. "The LORD is slow to anger, abounding in love and forgiving sin and rebellion" (Numbers 14:18).

- *is the fruit of His Spirit who indwells you.* As God dwells on the inside of you, He will produce His fruit in your life. "The fruit of the spirit is ... patience" (Galatians 5:22).

His understanding ...

- *is unlimited* (Psalm 147:5).

- *enabled Him to make the heavens and set them in place* (Psalm 136:5; Proverbs 3:19).

- *guards you* (Proverbs 2:11).

- *keeps you on a straight course* (Proverbs 15:21).

- *is a fountain of life* (Proverbs 16:22).

- *establishes your home* (Proverbs 24:3).

*It's the three pairs of eyes that mothers
have to have ... one pair that sees through
closed doors ... another in the back of her
head ... and, of course, the ones in front
that can look at a child when he goofs up
and reflect "I understand, and I love you"
without so much as uttering a word.*

ERMA BOMBECK
American Humorist

*Whoever is slow to anger
has great understanding.*

PROVERBS 14:29 NRSV

The Zipper

Engaged to be married at eighteen, I had stars in my eyes and gaping holes in my pockets. My job barely paid enough to keep gas and oil in my clunker of a car. My parents, struggling with finances themselves, would cover the costs of the reception but I'd be paying for my wedding gown. After scoping out the heart-stopping prices in various shops, I realized that if I wanted a pretty dress, I'd have to make it myself.

I found the perfect material in just the right shade of white, selected a beautiful pattern, and chose soft lace ribbons to accent the gown's flowing sleeves. Finally, I purchased a long white zipper to go down the back of the dress.

I couldn't wait to see the shining satin transformed into a beautiful wedding gown. Eagerly, I spread everything out on the bed and unfolded the paper pattern. Left bodice, right bodice, sleeves, neck lining, skirt—it looked like there were a million pieces! My head swam. Then Mother offered to help.

Sucking in a defiant breath, I brushed her aside. The pattern looked complicated, but I was confident I could handle it on my own.

"No, thanks," I told her. Mother only smiled in understanding and drifted out of my room.

The pattern pieces were soon pinned in place, and

my scissors flew as I cut through the fabric. Yards and yards of creamy white satin shimmered in my hands as I lovingly guided it beneath the flashing needles of the sewing machine. The pieces seemed to flow together, and even the sleeves went in smoothly. Before I knew it, it was time to sew in the zipper.

I pinned it into place and stitched slowly. The zipper skewed to one side. I picked out the threads one by one so as not to mar the delicate fabric and then re-pinned it and started over. Once again, the zipper fouled up.

Patiently, Mother hovered outside the room, silently watching. I knew she could sew zippers in all day long, flawlessly, and probably while blindfolded with one hand tied behind her back. But this was my dress, and I was going to do it all by myself, even if it killed me. I clenched my jaw and tackled the zipper again.

No matter how slowly I guided it through the machine, the zipper refused to go in straight. And now there were tiny holes in the satin from where I'd picked out the stitches! That was the last straw. I tossed the whole shining mess to the floor and stormed out of the house in tears.

After driving around for an hour or so, I finally calmed down, but every muscle in my body tensed when I stepped into my room to face the dreaded zipper again. However, instead of a mound of wrinkled, pin-pricked satin, I saw my beautiful wedding dress draped over a chair, the long white zipper sewn neatly in place. It nearly took my breath away.

I slipped the dress over my head and stood in front of the full-length mirror. Draped by folds of whispering satin, I caught a glimpse of Mother peeking around the door.

"Come in," I said, feeling suddenly shy. Even after the way I'd shoved her aside and refused her offer of help, she'd bailed me out of a terrible mess. How could she stand to look at me?

"The dress turned out great, didn't it?" she said, hugging me.

"Yes, it did!" I spun around, admiring the swirls of satin curving around my ankles and hugged her. "Thanks for sewing in the zipper."

She smiled, shook her head, and left the room, never to mention it again. Mother could have nagged me about my stubbornness, but she didn't. She could have scolded me for my attitude, but she let me be. She waited until I'd pushed things as far as I could, then she rescued me from myself, her patience and understanding conquering that stubborn long white zipper.[6] ♥

*It seems to me that my mother was the
most splendid woman I ever knew.
If I have amounted to anything,
it is due to her.*

CHARLIE CHAPLIN
Early Motion Picture Star Often Called "The
Funniest Man in the World"
1889-1977

The Love of a Mother

The love of a mother is never exhausted;

It never changes;

It never tires;

It endures through all,

In good repute, in bad repute;

In the face of the world's condemnation

A mother's love still lives on.

WASHINGTON IRVING
American Author
1783-1859

Through wisdom a house is built,
and by understanding it is established.

PROVERBS 24:3 NKJV

A mother's patience is like a tube of toothpaste—
it's never quite gone.

AUTHOR UNKNOWN

A Mother's Heart Is Prayerful and Vigilant

The power of one mother's prayers
could stand an army on its ear.

ELIZABETH DeHAVEN
Landscape Painter

As a mother, you have been given a powerful weapon—and the authority to use it on behalf of your child. This weapon is not limited by distance or time or physical strength. Lack of eloquence will not curb its effectiveness. It cannot be bought at any price. The woman who wields it needs have only one qualification—she must fully understand that she has been called to a task that is too big for her. To do and be and give your best to your children—you must be a mother who prays.

[Hannah said,] "I asked the LORD to give me this child, and he has given me my request. Now I am giving him to the LORD, and he will belong to the LORD his whole life."

1 SAMUEL 1:27-28 NLT

The most important occupation on earth for a woman is to be a real mother to her children. It does not have much glory to it; there is a lot of grit and grime. But there is no greater place of ministry, position, or power than that of a mother.

PHIL WHISENHUNT

God's Heart for Mothers Is Prayerful and Vigilant

❀ *He watches over you.* Any mother who has ever watched over a sleeping child knows the protective love that fills a mother's heart. In the same way God "will not let your foot slip—he who watches over you will not slumber ... nor sleep. The LORD watches over you— the LORD is your shade at your right hand; the sun will not harm you by day, nor the moon by night. The LORD will keep you from all harm—he will watch over your life; the LORD will watch over your coming and going both now and forevermore" (Psalm 121:3-8).

❀ *He hears you.* Just as the cry of your child brings you to his bedside to comfort him in the night, so "the eyes of the LORD are on the righteous and his ears are attentive to their cry" (Psalm 34:15).

❀ *You are on His mind.* Your beloved children remain in your heart from the moment you lay your eyes on them for the first time. God's heart is the same toward you: "See, I have engraved you on the palms of my hands; your walls are ever before me" (Isaiah 49:16).

❀ *Jesus intercedes for you.* As you pray for your children each day, know that Christ is also praying for you. "[Jesus] is able to save completely those who come to God through him, because he always lives to intercede for them" (Hebrews 7:25).

How sweet and happy seem those days of which I dream,

When memory recalls them now and then!

And with what rapture sweet

My weary heart would beat,

If I could hear my mother pray again.

If I could hear my mother pray again,

If I could hear her tender voice as then!

So glad I'd be, 'twould mean so much to me

If I could hear my mother pray again.

J. W. VAUGHAN

A Tribute to My Mother

I consider it a privilege to pray today for the one who has been praying for me all my life. Many times I caught her on her knees beside the rocker or the bed. And if I listened carefully, I would hear my name spoken. I would tiptoe away, careful not to disturb the holy conference being held in our simple home.

Now as I look back, I am touched deep in my soul by the love and constancy she demonstrated as she knelt there. Even now, Lord, well into old age, I see her lips move and her gaze lift as though she were looking into Your face. I know she prays for me still.

Make me sensitive to my mother, Lord, aware of her every need. Show me how to bless and care for her with equal fervor. And may she see all her prayers answered in my life.

Placed upon the Rock

O ur youngest son, Bob, was in the last year of high school when we felt we could go on an extended trip without him. So pulling our RV, we set out from California to visit relatives in Arkansas and Pennsylvania during my husband's vacation time from his teaching schedule.

Bob was a reliable young man. He and his friends spent many hours together, practicing guitar music, hiking in the mountains, or swimming in our backyard pool. While we were away, he was responsible for managing the household, and we had every confidence in his abilities.

One evening after arriving in Pennsylvania, I went to bed early in the RV. Suddenly, I awoke with an over-whelming desire to pray for my son. It was as if I battled the forces of evil ready to snatch him away from me.

"Lord God," I prayed, "protect my son! Wherever he is, whatever the circumstances, be near and help him." The urge to pray continued for several minutes. "Lord, there's nothing I can do to help my son, so I place him completely in Your hands. Take loving care of him."

The pressing need to pray lifted, and I finally drifted back to sleep. For months Bob kept secret what had happened to him during those desperate moments of prayer, but he finally broke down and told me.

He and his friend Ross decided to go snorkeling at Newport Beach that day. Ross called a weather-reporting agency and was told the day was mild with low undertow and clear visibility—perfect for snorkel diving.

By the time they reached their destination, much of the day had slipped away. The sandy beach where they entered the water looked beautiful, with small waves splashing against the shoreline. They swam out a good distance and dove, watching the fish swim among the seaweed. At one point Ross stopped to break open a sea urchin to feed the fish surrounding them, and that's when he noticed the water had turned turbulent and murky.

When the boys surfaced a few moments later, they decided the conditions looked risky and agreed to swim back to shore. Since the riptide had increased, Ross suggested climbing out of the water at a place where rocks provided a break in the surf. With snorkels up and faces in the water, they approached the area, but progressed slowly, fighting the choppy current.

"We'd been swimming between two rows of rocks extending about one hundred yards, fifteen feet apart, like parallel lines," Bob said, "when suddenly, I could feel my fins hit the bottom. Thinking we were near the shore, I stood up. The undercurrent was so strong the water had been drawn from beneath my feet. We were surrounded by high curling waves, forming a tunnel of water around us. The water that had been sucked up was now going to collapse. The only thing I could think of was, 'Okay, God, here we go.' I was literally spinning around underwater, holding my head to protect myself from the rocks."

While being buffeted from side to side in what appeared to be an impossible situation, Bob silently cried out for God's help. The next thing he remembers after that is rolling on his side on top of a giant rock. He got to his feet and realized he had been thrown completely out of the water and was standing on a cliff well above the surf line.

"I was down in that treacherous water," he said, "and God swept me up and placed me in a safe place, high upon a rock." As he gazed at the hazardous turbulence below him, he remembered Ross. "Lord," he prayed, "please save Ross too!"

A short time later, Ross approached him, and the two hugged as they rejoiced in being alive. Although they were both bruised and Bob had an abrasion to his knee, they were otherwise physically okay.

After Bob finished his story, I checked the calendar and realized that God had awakened me to pray at the very moment my son was in danger. I'm convinced the Lord has placed mothers on this earth to pray for their children, and God knows He can wake me up anytime![6] ❤

Mother's Love is like an island
In life's ocean, vast and wide,
A peaceful quiet shelter
From the wind and rain and tide.

Above it like a beacon light
Shone faith and truth and prayer;
And through the changing scenes of life,
I find a haven there.

AUTHOR UNKNOWN

Prayer is the application of the heart to God,
and the internal exercise of love.

SAMUEL TAYLOR COLERIDGE

English Poet

1772-1834

No nation ever had a better friend than the mother
who taught her children to pray.

AUTHOR UNKNOWN

A Mother's Heart Is Diligent and Determined

A man's work is from sun to sun,
but a mother's work is never done.

AUTHOR UNKNOWN

No one works more hours than a mother—not a soldier in combat, a doctor doing a double shift, or a fireman who stays until every ember has been extinguished. No matter how much time they might spend on the job, they all go home at some point, punch out, sign off—but not a mom. For eighteen years or so, she does back-to-back shifts with only an occasional break and only if someone can be found to cover her bases for a few hours. After that and for the rest of her life, she's on call. Still in all, motherhood always has been and will continue to be the best job on earth!

Diligent hands bring wealth.

PROVERBS 10:4

*Over the centuries [mothers have] worked as hard as fathers
and for very different reasons.
He has built the houses; she's added the colors, the smells, the music.
He has shaped constitutions to make citizens protected;
she has sewn flags to make them weep and cheer.
He has mustered armies and police forces to put down oppression;
she has prayed for them and patted them on the back and
sent them off with their heads up.
He has shaped decisions; she has added morale.
Celebrate the mother! She, too, no less than the father, has, under
God, shaped a magnificent human tradition.[7]*

ANNE ORTLUND
Christian Speaker and Author

Mother

She carried me under her heart;

Loved me before I was born;

Took God's hand in hers and walked through the

Valley of Shadows

that I might live.

She bathed me when I was helpless

Clothed me when I was naked;

Gave me warm milk from her own body

when I was hungry.

She rocked me to sleep when I was weary;

Pillowed me on pillows softer than down,

And sang to me in the voice of an Angel.

She held my hand when I learned to walk;

Suffered with my sorrow;

Laughed with my joy;

Glowed with my triumph; and while I knelt at her side,

she taught my lips to pray.

Through all the days of my youth, she gave

Strength for my weakness, courage for my despair,

and hope to fill my hopeless heart.

She was loyal when others failed;

True when tried by fire;

My friend when other friends were gone.

She prayed for me through all the days—

whether flooded with sunshine or saddened by shadows.

She loved me when I was unlovely,

and helped me to grow strong and wise.

Even if I should lay down my life for her,

I could never pay the debt I owe to my mother.

AUTHOR UNKNOWN

God's Heart for Mothers Is Diligent and Determined

God is diligent and determined ...

- ❀ *to watch over you.* Just as mothers lovingly and diligently watch over their children, "the eyes of the LORD are everywhere, keeping watch on the wicked and the good" (Proverbs 15:3).

- ❀ *to fulfill His Word.* If God has said it, He will do it! You can count on Him to keep His promises. "The LORD said to me, 'You have seen correctly, for I am watching to see that my word is fulfilled'" (Jeremiah 1:12).

- ❀ *never to fail.* You can count on God—He is trustworthy, and He will not fail you. "Everything he does reveals his glory and majesty. His righteousness never fails" (Psalm 111:3 NLT).

- ❀ *to help you in your time of need.* When a child cries out in the night, his mother rushes to see what he needs. In the same way, God wants to meet our needs as we come to Him in faith and make our requests known. "Let us then fearlessly and confidently and boldly draw near to the throne of grace ... that we may receive mercy ... and find grace ... [appropriate help and well-timed help, coming just when we need it]" (Hebrews 4:16 AMP).

A Single Mom to the Rescue

Over the years single mom Kathi Picton adopted three children—daughter Molly from a Korean, Native-, and African-American descent; Vanessa, an African-American daughter raised in the foster-care system; and Ryan, who was born with Down syndrome.

Not only is there no husband to brainstorm with on disciplinary issues, or strategies for finances, or the juggling of schedules, Kathi brings home the bacon, fries it up in the pan, washes the pan, puts it away, and replaces it when it breaks. She does all of this at an age when most women are looking forward to retirement, entertaining visions of golf courses and cruises to warm climates. Kathi will never retire because there are too many children in need, and she is determined to take care of as many as she can.

Her compassionate heart runs to children in need of rescue for two reasons: her brother, whom she adores, was born with Down syndrome, and her firstborn child was struck and killed by a car three decades ago at just six years of age.

Kathi rescued Ryan as an infant and now works diligently as his advocate with school departments and state agencies and employers. When Ryan finds it difficult to speak or articulate his ideas, Kathi becomes his voice and his protector.

Her adopted daughter Vanessa had languished for years in the foster-care system. By the age of nine, the little girl had bounced from one family to another eight times, with her last placement being in a group home. Despite having concerned caretakers, nothing could take the place of knowing a loving mother was keeping watch over her. So the little girl waited.

Kathi discovered Vanessa through books in the library where foster children could be viewed. Eventually after months of home visits and evaluations, Vanessa came to live permanently with Kathi, arriving on the scene with little fanfare and carrying one small possession—a small cardboard box that held some clothes and a few favorite toys and gifts from the staff at her group home.

There were no baby pictures, as if that part of her life journey never really existed, but some thoughtful person had tucked in an envelope containing pictures of her most recent years. Along with the box and the pictures, the little girl came with a resiliency and survival instinct buried deep inside.

Kathi provided Vanessa's last stop in search of a permanent home. The first year was rocky, but as Kathi continually showed Vanessa how much she loved her, they developed a close mother-daughter relationship. Trust grew between them, like a palpable presence as they walked through trials and battles and late-night conversations filled with promises that would be kept.

As Vanessa proved that she could handle more responsibility and freedom, Kathi gave her more and more privilege. And Vanessa gave Kathi her heart when she finally realized that she had come home. Kathi was different. She was a mother with a mother's heart—not just a caretaker.

Kathi's devotion to children and her desire to go above and beyond the call of duty to help little ones, especially those the Bible calls "the least of these," is a testament of God's calling on her life. Her quiet strength, her diligence and determination, were forged by treading on some of life's most dreary, desolate, and frightening roads. She has faced lost relationships and failed dreams and survived. Instead of bitterness, it bred in her compassion.

Kathi took a truckload of grief from her own past and corralled all the emotion to serve others, using it to change the direction of some nearly derailed young people who were fortunate enough to walk across the path of one of God's grandest creations—a "true mother."[8] ❤

My mother, whose disposition was always bright and optimistic, was active, energetic and wholly devoted to her large family. No sacrifice was too great, no task too hard, for her willing heart and hands. Her work was hard and her hours long. Only God knows the number of nights she walked the floor, rocked the cradle, or sat by the bedside of her children during their many, many ailments.

OSWALD J. SMITH
Pastor Best Known for His Passion for Missions
1889-1986

The phrase "working mother" is redundant.

JANE SELLMAN
Romance Author

Always give yourselves fully to the work of the Lord,

because you know that your labor

in the Lord is not in vain.

1 CORINTHIANS 15:58

A Mother's Heart Is Gentle and Forgiving

The heart of a mother is a deep abyss at the bottom of which
you will always discover forgiveness.

HONORE DE BALZAC
French Novelist
1799-1850

Two of the virtues most often attributed to mothers are gentleness and forgiveness. And really this is no surprise. God has endowed you and all mothers with those characteristics, because He knew it was in a child's nature to transgress. If your hand did not tremble slightly at the mere touch of your child's face—often even after they've become adults—you might find your mercy spent too quickly. If you could not divest yourself of anger and resentment almost instantaneously, how could you stay focused on your task for even a day? Relish these gifts, use them often and well. They are the very tools you need to do God's work.

[Your beauty] ... should be that of your inner self,

the unfading beauty of a gentle and quiet spirit,

which is of great worth in God's sight.

1 PETER 3:3,4

Look in those eyes ... Listen to that dear voice ...
Notice the feeling of even a single touch that is
bestowed upon you by that gentle hand!
Make much of it while yet you have that most precious
of all gifts. Read the unfathomable love of those eyes;
the anxiety of that tone and look, however slight is
your pain. In after life you may have friends, fonds,
dears, but never you will have again the inexpressible
love and gentleness lavished upon you which
none but a mother bestows.

FRANCIS MACAULAY
English Mathematician
1862-1937

Two Mothers

Long, long ago, so I have been told,
Two saints once met on the streets paved with gold.
"By the stars in your crown," said the one
to the other,
"I see that on earth, you too were a mother;
And by the blue-tinted halo you wear,
You too have known sorrow and deepest despair."
"Ah yes," came the answer, "I once had a son,
A sweet little lad, full of laughter and fun."

"But tell of your child—" "Oh, I knew I was blest
From the moment I first held him close to my
breast;
And my heart almost burst with the joy of that
day."
"Ah yes," sighed the other, "I felt the same way."
The former continued, "The first steps he took—
"So eager and breathless; the sweet, startled look

Which came over his face—he trusted me so—"
"Yes," sighed the other, "how well do I know!"

"But soon he had grown to a tall handsome boy,
So stalwart and kind, and it gave me such joy
To have him just walk down the street by my side."
"Ah yes," said the other, "I felt the same pride.
How often I shielded and spared him from pain;
And when he, for others, was cruelly slain,
When they crucified him and they spat in his face,
How gladly would I have hung there in His place!"

A moment of silence—"Oh, then you are she,
The mother of Christ?" and she fell on one knee,
But Mary raised her up, drawing her near,
And kissed from the cheek of the woman—a tear.
"Tell me the name of your son you loved so,
That I may share your grief and your woe."
She lifted her eyes, looking straight at the other,
"He was Judas Iscariot! I am his mother!"

AUTHOR UNKNOWN

God's Heart for Mothers Is Gentle and Forgiving

A mother's heart is gentle, caring for her children tenderly and with great concern. A mother's love, like God's, is endlessly forgiving, committed to her children no matter what they might do.

❋ "See, your king comes to you, righteous and having salvation, gentle and riding on a donkey, on a colt, the foal of a donkey" (Zechariah 9:9).

❋ Jesus said, "Come to me, all you who are weary and burdened, and I will give you rest. Take my yoke upon you and learn from me, for I am gentle and humble in heart, and you will find rest for your souls. For my yoke is easy and my burden is light" (Matthew 11:28-30).

❋ Jesus said, "This is my blood of the covenant, which is poured out for many for the forgiveness of sins" (Matthew 26:28).

❋ "If you, O LORD, kept a record of sins, O Lord, who could stand? But with you there is forgiveness; therefore you are feared" (Psalm 130:3-4).

❋ "The LORD, the LORD, the compassionate and gracious God, slow to anger, abounding in love and faithfulness, maintaining love to thousands, and forgiving wickedness, rebellion and sin" (Exodus 34:6-7).

A mother is the person who sits up with
you when you are sick, and puts up with
you when you are well.

AUTHOR UNKNOWN

[Mothers] have a heart that never hardens,
a temper that never tires,
and a touch that never hurts.

CHARLES DICKENS
Great English Novelist
1812-1870

A Tribute to My Mother

When I reach back to my earliest memory, back as far as I can go, she was there—my mother—lifting me to my feet after I'd fallen. Even then, she was looking past my mistakes, brushing me off, and encouraging me to try again. Through the years, I can't count the times she has given me the courage and the confidence to get back on my feet after a bout of poor judgment, naiveté, or just plain willfulness.

Lord, Your blessing is already on her—I know that. She wears it like a beautiful lace shawl, covering her head and her shoulders. But Lord, I ask that You bless her even more. Forgive her for her mistakes as freely and as perfectly as she has forgiven me throughout the years. And reward her for all her noble deeds. Help her to feel the warmth of my love and gratitude every day of her life.

Those Hands I Love

Three rambunctious boys! How could a mother be expected to keep up with us? Yet we lived carefree and happy, growing up in one of the faded clapboard houses that sat facing the road on either side of the "Big House" on the Whitehall Plantation just west and across the wide Mississippi from Natchez.

Mom worked in the grade school cafeteria; and though it was probably illegal then as now, often we ate leftovers from the day's lunch for our supper. We always had fish sticks on Saturday, left from Friday's Catholic-friendly fare. There was plenty of out-of-date milk in little waxed cartons to fill us up. Mama couldn't bear to throw it out. It kept us alive during that lean time.

Mom managed beans and cornbread, turnip greens, rice and fried fish, and potatoes for us. Still she worked full time between the school and helping Dad run the store.

One day right at dusk, Mom pulled into the drive. We had been fishing at the bar pits along the levee. David had just caught a nice fish and ran with it still on his line and pole to show the folks.

He ran shouting: "Hey, look what a good big 'un I got!" straight across the road and straight into the path of a gin pole truck.

Brakes squealed, tires screeched, but the truck was heavy and too close. It was too late. I watched in motionless horror as the truck smacked into David and his thin body flew some fifty feet forward and landed in the ditch jerking our world to a deathly stop.

A scream on her lips, Mom came running. The trucker jumped out and ran—horror twisting his face. A neighbor who had a phone ran inside to call for help and after long minutes that seemed endless, the ambulance came roaring up—sirens blaring.

The medics gathered David up and carried him to the ambulance and backed out with Mom in the back beside him. The rest of us stood paralyzed with fear— the sudden look at death all too close was unthinkable.

The neighbor lady, Mrs. Wagner, shepherded us into her house and sat us at the table for a meal we couldn't eat.

David was not dead, but his pelvis, his legs, nearly every bone in his lower body had been broken. His cheek was torn and the bones of his jaw broken. His thin eight-year-old body was covered with cuts and bruises and grated by gravel. The blow to his head left him unconscious.

For the next twenty-eight days Mom sat beside her boy, gently comforting him, watching over his silence, praying for God's mercy. Then one glorious day he stirred, opened his eyes, and from a throat the doctors had warned her would likely never speak again came that wonderful, beautiful word: "Mama."

The coma was over and David slipped back into life. "He may never improve; he'll never be normal—never make it out of a wheelchair." All these predictions proved wrong, with Mama's loving attention and her tender care, David recovered. He would learn to talk and to walk all over again.

For six weeks he endured a full body cast from his chest to the ankle on one leg and to the knee of the other. He could shimmy around on his belly inside the house. His cast soon grew dirty. After six weeks the doctors removed the cast and, finding the leg bones still unhealed, they incarcerated him for another six-week term.

We brothers were relegated to near slavery, toting David around outside in a Red Ryder wagon wherever he commanded and transporting toys, pets, food, and drink to His Royal Majesty.

Mom looked on and laughed. After the second cast came off, the tedious rehab began. Mom taught her son to walk again, to tie his shoes, and finally to climb. She worked with him to help him overcome his fear of running and playing, of being a real boy again, of going back to school.

The hands of my mother now shake when she pours a cup of coffee or tries to ladle soup. Her once lovely handwriting is not clear and smooth, but jerky and hard to decipher—but those gentle hands that nursed me and my brothers, that fed, that guided, led, and loved ... I love those hands.[9] ❤

God's Masterpiece Is Mother

God took the fragrance of a flower

The majesty of a tree

The gentleness of morning dew

The calm of a quiet sea

The beauty of the twilight hour

The soul of a starry night

The laughter of a rippling brook

The grace of a bird in flight

Then God fashioned from these things

A creation like no other,

And when his masterpiece was through

He called it simply—Mother.

HERBERT FARNHAM

American Poet

*I love my mother for all the times she said absolutely nothing.
... I thank her for all her virtues, but mostly for never once
having said, "I told you so."*

ERMA BOMBECK
American Humorist
1927-1996

*God pardons like a mother,
who kisses the offense into everlasting forgetfulness.*

HENRY WARD BEECHER
Eloquent, Dramatic, and Witty Protestant Preacher
1813-1887

A Mother's Heart Is God's Temple

Of all earthly music, that which reaches farthest into heaven is the beating of a truly loving heart.

HENRY WARD BEECHER
Eloquent, Dramatic, and Witty Protestant Preacher
1813-1887

A child in the womb takes the best that its mother's body has to offer. The nutrients she takes in go first to the small life inside, her body receiving only the leftovers. Her heart pumps the baby's blood, her lungs provide it with oxygen, her digestive system processes its food. A mother's body serves as a refuge for that new life and as such becomes a temple dedicated to God's service. How amazing! How miraculous!

[O LORD,] it was you who formed
my inward parts; you knit me together in
my mother's womb.

PSALM 139:13 NRSV

A mother is a chalice, the vessel
without which no human being has ever been born.
She is created to be a life-bearer, cooperating with
her husband and with God in the making of a child.
What a solemn responsibility. What an unspeakable
privilege—a vessel divinely prepared
for the Master's use.

ELISABETH ELLIOT
Best-Selling Author and Bible Teacher

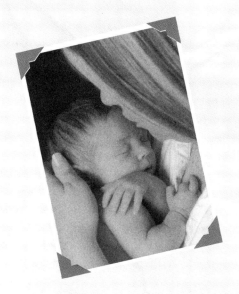

Mother

You painted no Madonnas
On chapel walls in Rome,
But with a touch diviner
You lived one in your home.

You wrote no lofty poems
That critics counted art,
But with a nobler vision
You lived them in your heart.

You carved no shapeless marble
To some high soul design,
But with a finer sculpture
You shaped this soul of mine.

You built no great cathedrals
That centuries applaud,
But with a grace exquisite
Your life cathedraled God.

Had I the gift of Raphael
Or Michelangelo,
Oh, what a rare Madonna
My mother's life would show.

THOMAS W. FESSENDEN

God's Heart for Mothers Is to Live in Them

Because God lives in you …

❀ *He walks the earth today.* God lives inside of you, and everything you do and every word you say is the loving expression of God to your children. "We are the temple of the living God. As God has said: 'I will live with them and walk among them, and I will be their God, and they will be my people'" (2 Corinthians 6:16).

❀ *you have a significant role to play.* There are many roles a woman will play in her lifetime, but undoubtedly, the role of mother is one of the most challenging. Rest assured that God has called you to this role and will give you the grace needed to accomplish it. "Just as each of us has one body with many members, and these members do not all have the same function, so in Christ we who are many form one body, and each member belongs to all the others. We have different gifts, according to the grace given us" (Romans 12:4-6).

❀ *you are able to walk in His ways.* As you live out God's love before your children, they will come to know Him in a deeper way. "I will give you a new heart and put a new spirit in you; I will remove from you your heart of stone and give you a heart of flesh. And I will put my Spirit in you and move you to follow my decrees and be careful to keep my laws" (Ezekiel 36:26-27).

A Tribute to My Mother

Thank You Father, for my mother. Before I was born, she carried me in her womb. When I was small and helpless, she carried me in her arms. Now that I'm grown, she carries me in her heart. I owe her my life, and that is just the beginning.

I ask today that You would decorate her life with blessings fitting of Your temple. Return to her what she has so willingly given to me—love, kindness, forgiveness, understanding, hope, faith, and so much more. Let this day be a special day of celebration—a day to stop, remember, and give thanks for the wonderful person she is.

A Temple of God's Love

It had always been difficult for my mother to reveal her emotions—those things buried deep inside her soul that were most important to her.

One night Mother came to hear me say my prayers: "Now I lay me down to sleep. I pray the Lord my soul to keep. If I should die before I wake, I pray the Lord my soul to take."

"Mom," I asked, "what's God like? Can He really hear me? Where is He? Why can't I see Him?" The questions came fast—so many things I wondered about. "Where did I come from? How did I get here, Mom?"

My questions soon died away. There were so many things she could not talk about. I knew instinctively that I had trespassed on her deep and private soul.

"Love" was one of those words she could not say. The word was never used at our house. Papa cradled and cuddled me in his big arms, and I knew that he loved me. But Mom was unable to even show affection.

As I entered my teens, Mother began to consult me about many things. She let me choose the patterns for my dresses and taught me how to sew.

On the day before I left for college, I came home to a table set with the best dishes. The delicious aroma of fried chicken filled the air, and a beautiful cake with coconut frosting graced the center of the table.

"Mom, is the preacher coming for supper?" I asked.

"No," she answered with one of her rare sweet smiles. "It's just the three of us."

Suddenly, I knew. I was the special guest. It was her going-away gift of love to me. There could never be a single shred of doubt again. My mother loved me!

I was a junior in college when the superintendent of the school I had attended during high school called and offered me a position as a teacher in the elementary school. I was delighted with the job offer and asked only that I be allowed to finish the last three weeks of the semester so that I would not lose my credits. I planned to go to summer school to earn my bachelor's degree.

It was during spring break in my third year of teaching that Mom began to hemorrhage. We rushed her to a hospital and waited anxiously for a diagnosis.

"Leukemia," pronounced the doctor. "There's no known cure for it at this time. However, with treatment, she could live for two years or even as many as ten."

We were heartbroken. Mother was rushed off to a Memphis hospital where she received treatment, and soon the dreaded disease was in remission. When she returned home, she seemed in good spirits and almost like her former self. But she tired easily.

One day I came in from school to find her absorbed in writing a series of letters, "T. L. I. M. S, I. S. N. W. ..."

"What are you doing?" I asked.

"I'm packing my suitcase," she answered softly. "You know I must go away soon. I'm memorizing Psalm 23 and Psalm 121. It's hard for me to memorize since I've been sick, so I write down the first letter of each word and I keep going over and over it until I've learned it."

A transformation had taken place, and now that her time with us was short, she began to reveal her inner self. Then she told me about a woman who had come to visit her while she was in the hospital.

"She read scriptures to me, and it helped me so much," Mother said, "but I know the time will come when I won't be able to hear anyone reading to me. So you see, I'm packing my suitcase."

The time did come when my mother lay in a coma in a hospital bed, unresponsive to those around her. The words of the twenty-third Psalm rang in my heart, "Yea, though I walk through the valley of the shadow of death, I will fear no evil, for Thou art with me."

There was a shining peace in the room when Mother died. It was her last gift to me, a gift of comfort and peace to hold me steady through all the days to come. Even though she still could not share it verbally, I knew her heart had always been a temple of God's love.[10] ❤

*Even Jesus who died for us upon the Cross,
in the last hour, in the unutterable agony of
death, was mindful of His mother, as if to
teach us that this holy love should be our
last worldly thought—the last point
of earth from which the soul should
take its flight for heaven.*

HENRY WADSWORTH LONGFELLOW
English Poet
1807-1882

When God thought of mother, he must have laughed with satisfaction and framed it quickly—so rich, so deep, so divine, so full of soul, power, and beauty was the conception.

HENRY WARD BEECHER
Eloquent, Dramatic, and Witty Protestant Preacher
1813-1887

Many women have done wonderful things, but you've outclassed them all!

PROVERBS 31:29 THE MESSAGE

ENDNOTES

1. Renie Burghardt. Used by permission of the author.
2. Charlotte Adelsperger. Used by permission of the author.
3. Kathryn Lay. Used by permission of the author.
4. Rosie Braatz. Used by permission of the author.
5. Anne C. Watkins. Used by permission of the author.
6. Loretta Miller Mehl. Used by permission of the author.
7. Anne Ortlund, *Disciplines of the Home.* (Nashville, TN, Word Publishing, 1990).
8. Linda MacKillop. Used by permission.
9. C. E. Hollis. Used by permission.
10. Margaret Maghe. Used by permission.

This and other titles in the Celebration Series
are available from your local bookstore.

Celebrate Love
Celebrate the Graduate
Celebrate Dads

If this book has touched your life,
we would love to hear from you.
Please send your comments to:
editorialdept@whitestonebooks.com
Visit our website at:
www.whitestonebooks.com

*"... To him who overcomes I will give some of the hidden manna to
eat. And I will give him a white stone, and on the stone a new name
written which no one knows except him who receives it."*

REVELATION 2:17 NKJV

WHITE STONE BOOKS
LAKELAND, FLORIDA